MOODS OF COUNTY DURHAM

First published in Great Britain in 2006

Title page: Durham Cathedral and the Old Fulling Mill in summer.
A few years ago a group of trees were cleared from the steep bank above
South Street Mill revealing, across the river, what was to become
popularly known as 'The New View'.

British Library Cataloguing-in-Publication Data
A CIP record for this title is available from the British Library

ISBN 1 84114 561 0
ISBN 978 1 84114 561 7

HALSGROVE
Halsgrove House
Lower Moor Way
Tiverton, Devon EX16 6SS
T: 01884 243242
F: 01884 243325
email: sales@halsgrove.com
website: www.halsgrove.com

Printed and bound by D'Auria Industrie Grafiche Spa, Italy

MOODS OF
COUNTY DURHAM

PHILIP NIXON

HALSGROVE

Acknowledgements

Thanks to my family, my wife Val who has made a valuable input, my son Mark who is an extremely competent photographer in his own right, my daughter Sophy who gave her wonderful artistic talent in drawing the map; for all their valued support and patience in the production of this work. Not forgetting Archie the labrador whose company on walks has been most enjoyable.

Simon Butler, Marie Lewis and Karen Binaccioni of Halsgrove who have been the most dedicated, hardworking publishing support group an author could wish for. Thank you!

Baldersdale in Winter – Hury Reservoir and Goldsborough.

Introduction

County Durham is the only English county that is not a shire. The Irish styling of its name distinguishes it from the rest of England and it therefore retains, at least in name, the status of a County Palatine. By reason of its distance from London it was ruled for eight hundred years by a succession of Prince Bishops whose influence on the development of the County, and, indeed, the whole of the ancient Kingdom of Northumbria, has been immense.

It is a county of great contrasts. Once it was a heavily industrialised area and, indeed, was at the forefront of the Industrial Revolution. It is one of the few counties in England that has become more rural over the last few years, helped by the long-remembered local government boundary changes of 1974 which effectively moved the county further south, taking in some of North Yorkshire on the south bank of the River Tees but losing some of the industrial areas of Stockton-on-Tees and Wearside, particularly the city, or town, as it was then, of Sunderland and the town of Gateshead.

The eastern border of the county is the North Sea and its dramatic and beautiful coastline with its unique 'Denes' – deep, richly wooded, and often secluded valleys that wind down to the seashore. The north and south boundaries roughly follow the valleys of the Derwent and Tyne in the north and the valley of the mighty River Tees in the south. To the west are the North Pennine Hills, one of the last wild places in England and now designated an Area of Outstanding Natural Beauty. The whole of this beautiful landscape is centered on the City of Durham and the World Heritage Site with its impressive Castle and magnificent Cathedral sited on the small, easily defendable, rocky peninsula formed by a loop in the River Wear.

During the most productive times of coal mining the Durham coast suffered because some collieries tipped their waste into the sea, and a huge amount was washed ashore and polluted the beaches. This has all changed. A massive clean-up and regeneration programme has seen vast improvement and the reclaimed natural beauty of this naturally rugged area is now enjoyed by many visitors, walkers and cyclists.

Since the decline in industrialisation in the middle of the county a lot of the land has been reclaimed and used as farmland which has enhanced the rural aspect of the county. Coal mines once worked within the boundaries of Durham City but tourism, smaller hi-tech industries and agriculture are now all flourishing occupations. A lot of the disused railway lines in the area have been put to use as convenient and comfortable paths for cycling and walking, allowing easy access to the countryside.

On the western side of County Durham are the dales of Derwentside, Weardale, Teesdale, Lunedale, Baldersdale and Gretadale; each one is different in aspect from its neighbour but all are part of the North Pennines Area of Outstanding Natural Beauty. This part of the county was also industrialised. Lead mining was an important industry in the hills surrounding these dales in Victorian times and there is much evidence of the massive workings that have changed the landscape. The remains of great hushes, level mouths, railways, houseteads, mineshops, bridge abutments and pack horse trails are all being slowly regained and mellowed by nature.

Drystone walls discipline the hillsides but visually link the houses, byres and field barns which are still set apart. The quarries from which the stones were taken for these rural buildings are now silent havens of peace and tranquillity. The beautiful hay meadows are flourishing once again and in spring and early summer the road verges and fields burst into a mesmerising display of wildflowers and grasses.

Harsh weather also adds a certain attraction to this interesting landscape but in this part of the county the winters can be harsh and long – the North Pennine wind whips down the valleys, carving and sculpting the snow into dynamic shapes – the scene is transformed so much that sometimes it is hard to tell where the land ends and the sky begins – it sometimes seems that winter will never end, but it does and with the onset of spring the whole cycle starts again.

County Durham is an area of infinite variety and its photographic possibilities are such that the difficulty arises in not what to include but in what to leave out! I have tried in this selection to reflect both the mood and the variety in the County and feel privileged that I have been commissioned to present this personal selection.

I have been fortunate enough to be a professional photographer for most of my working life and to be asked to make a personal selection of photographs of my home County must rank as one of the most satisfying of commissions.

A variety of cameras have been used to produce the images for this book – medium format SLRs, 35mm SLRs and compacts plus digital SLRs. Lenses used have ranged from super-wide angle through to super-telephoto, filters were used where necessary; the film was mostly Fuji or Kodak, and the tripod was heavy!

Philip Nixon ARPS, LMPA, DipPP

County Durham

The beach and north pier at Seaham in the early morning light. The harbour was founded by Lord Londonderry in 1828 to export the coal from his nearby collieries.

The North Sea demonstrating its awesome power; a huge wave crashes over the lighthouse on the north pier at Seaham.

Seaham Beach in a calm twilight.

The promenade on the seafront at Seaham dates from those Victorian days when it was considered both healthy and fashionable to 'take the sea-air'.

The north and south piers enclose the harbour at Seaham.

The clifftop park at Seaham in summer – regeneration has been high on the agenda since the disappearance of coal-mining in County Durham.

Lord Londonderry's statue in pride of place in front of the old police station which has been tastefully converted into luxury sea-front apartments.

The small north harbour provides a quiet haven for fishing boats.

St Mary's is the oldest church in Seaham and dates from Saxon and Norman times. The short-lived marriage between Anne Isabella Milbanke and Lord Byron took place in what was her father's nearby Seaham Hall in 1815. Their signatures are recorded in the church register.

Dawdon Beach near Seaham is where local collieries tipped their waste into the sea; this beach was featured in the final scene of the classic British film *Get Carter*

Hawthorn Hive, the attractive little bay at the mouth of Hawthorn Dene, belies the presence of a dangerous reef – 'the Skaw' – which projects into the sea here and in the nineteenth century claimed many ships and the lives of their mariners. The worst year, according to historian and traveller John Murray, was 1824 when fifty ships and their crews were lost.

Cattle grazing in the early morning on Beacon Hill, the highest point on the Durham Coast.

County Durham has an impressive rugged coastline, dotted with secluded bays and inlets.

A coastal footpath has been developed over the last few years offering the opportunity for bracing clifftop walks.

Overlooking Foxholes Dene near Easington. A rich variety of wildflowers can be found along the coast during the summer months.

The impressive Victorian railway viaduct carries the Sunderland-to-Hartlepool coastal railway high above Castle Eden Dene Mouth.

Castle Eden Dene. These Denes are a special feature of the Durham Coast – steep-sided deep, tree-covered valleys, eroded by streams and small rivers in the soft limestone flowing to the sea. These secluded shady places are wonderful for peaceful walks to enjoy the plants and flowers.

Bathers take advantage of a fine day on Blackhall Beach.

Derwent Reservoir was opened in 1967 and is a favourite leisure location.
There are several picnic areas and a sailing club on its shores.

Derwentcote Steel Furnace dates from 1721 and produced, along with several other furnaces in the area, the excellent 'Newcastle Steel' that enjoyed a reputation of being superior quality.

Sedgefield is a small market town built around a village green where the traditional Shrove Tuesday football match is still played.

The church of St Mary Magadalene in Trimdon village was founded by Augustinian monks from Guisborough Priory who farmed nearby. Trimdon takes its name from 'Tremadune' – 'the cross on the hill'. Unfortunately no records of this early settlement exist because they were burnt in revenge by a monk who was dismissed from Guisborough.

The remains of the Bishop's Castle and hunting park at Bishop Middleham. The Bishop of Durham had a castle and an extensive hunting park here from the twelfth to the fourteenth centuries.

The Gothic gatehouse in Hardwick Hall Park was built as a folly by John Burdon of Hardwick Hall. The hall is now an hotel but has seen use as a maternity home among other things. The recently reconstructed country park is now returned to its former glory and is expertly administered by Durham County Council.

St Helen's Church in Kelloe dates from Norman times and is picturesquely sited on the north bank of Kelloe Beck. The church has strong connections with Elizabeth Barrett Browning – she was baptised here and lived in the nearby, but now demolished, Coxhoe Hall.

Kelloe Miners' Memorial stands as a poignant reminder of a dreadful mining tragedy – it marks the burial place of 26 of the 74 men and boys who lost their lives in the Trimdon Grange Colliery explosion on 16 February 1882.

Renny's Lane, in Gilesgate on the edge of Durham City, is an ancient footpath that links the city with the village of Sherburn – it connects with the trackbed of the old Belmont Colliery-to-Pittington railway.

Cattle and sheep make the most of the evening grazing on the rolling countryside near Quarrington Hill.

Tanfield railway is manned by dedicated enthusiasts and recreates the mood, the feel, and the even the nostalgic scent, of the days of steam engines.

Causey Arch is believed to be the world's oldest surviving railway bridge – however it is said that its designer, Ralph Wood, jumped to his death from the bridge because he feared it would collapse.

Finchale Priory is regarded as Durham's finest monastic ruin and is closely associated with St Godric. He spent his time in this 'snake-infested' spot as a hermit. He used a stone for a pillow, would only eat food when it was rotten, and would bake ashes from the fire into his bread. He furthered his penance by praying while standing up to his neck in ice-cold water. In spite of this tremendous asceticism he lived to be 105 years old. Eventually a church was built here and the monks of Durham would come here four at a time on a rota system to stay with the five resident monks – it became known as 'a holiday home for the monks of Durham'.

Waldridge Fell is crossed with many interlinking footpaths; the area is unique in Durham because it is the only low level heath at sea level in the county.

Whitworth Hall walled garden. Whitworth Hall is now an hotel but it was once the home of the handsome Robert Shafto – man of fashion and MP for Durham – whose name lives on in the famous northern ballad:

Bobby Shafto's gone to sea
Silver buckles on his knee;
He'll come back and marry me,
Bonnie Bobby Shafto.

He didn't, of course, and supposedly broke the heart of poor Bridget, the daughter of Sir Henry Bellasis, Lord of the nearby Brancepeth Castle.

Beamish Woods in
soft in autumn light.

The Weardale Way points to Chester-le-Street – St Cuthbert's body rested here for 113 years during his epic journey from Lindisfarne to Durham; during that time Chester-le-Street became the centre of Christianity in the north.

Houghall Woods. Every spring the bluebells put on a magnificent display in this mature woodland, close to the centre of Durham City.

Kepier Wood is reputedly where some of the stone used for the building of Durham Cathedral was quarried. There were also extensive coal mining drifts here in the early twentieth century – all the industrial workings have now gone leaving only a series of secluded winding woodland paths.

St Margaret's Chapel dates from around the mid 1400s and was built as the chapel of a small hospital founded to care for the poor, the infirm, and those who had fallen on hard times in the Gilesgate area.

Durham Castle, from the main gate, in the early spring, with a wonderful fresh display of daffodils and forsythia.

Durham Castle from the riverside path near South Street Mill during a late frost in spring.

A morning mist lingers around the river banks in Durham City.

Prebends' Bridge, almost hidden by a freezing mist on a cold winter's morning.

Framwellgate Bridge and the
western towers of Durham Cathedral
from Milburngate riverside

Durham Cathedral as seen from St Margaret's Churchyard. The houses are part of South Street, one of the city's most sought-after addresses.

The central and western towers of Durham Cathedral seen from South Street through a tracery of backlit autumn leaves. The huge, magnificent Norman building presents many different aspects from all over the city and its environs, each season or time of day offering what seems to be an inexhaustible variety of views in different lighting effects.

The central towers and eastern spires of Durham Cathedral as seen from New Elvet Bridge. The houses in the foreground are on Old Elvet Bridge.

Early morning in Autumn. The Chapel of the Nine Altars and the Rose Window at the eastern end of Durham Cathedral.

The Central Tower of Durham Cathedral
from The Palace Green.

Bright morning sunshine creates a strong pattern of arch shadows in the Cloisters of Durham Cathedral.

Ponies enjoy the early winter sunshine near the village of Edmundbyers, Derwentside.

A stand of Scots pines near Muggleswick.

Feeding sheep on Muggleswick Common. Sheep farming is hard work, especially in winter when food has to be taken to the animals on the fells.

Pow Hill Country Park on the shores of Derwent Reservoir – an approaching storm sends visitors scurrying for the shelter of their cars.

The still surface of Derwent Reservoir, disturbed only by a single small boat.

Farmland, near the small hamlet of Hollinside, in late summer.

The churchyard at Escomb
has no corners in which the
devil could hide...

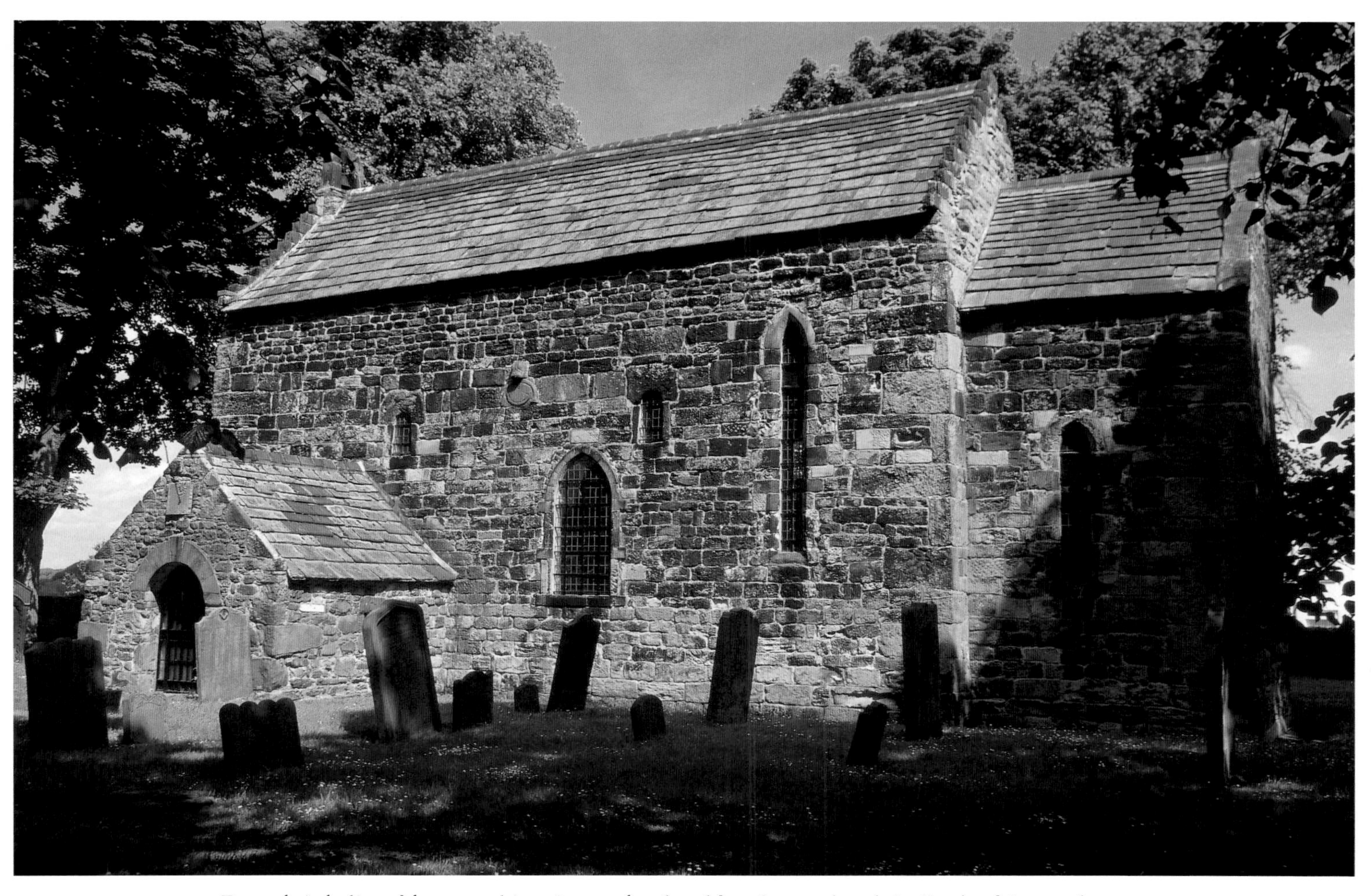

Escomb is believed by some historians to be the oldest Saxon church in England in regular use.

Auckland Castle dates from the twelfth century and since the time of Bishop William van Mildert (1826-1836) has been the official residence of The Bishop of Durham. Prior to that date it served as a country residence, used by the bishop and his associates for hunting.

The market town of Crook, with its modern Civic Centre, seen from Dowfold Hill. It is said that the Devil's Stones in the market place were hurled from this very spot by the devil himself – a much more romantic story than the geological explanation describing them as glacial erratics!

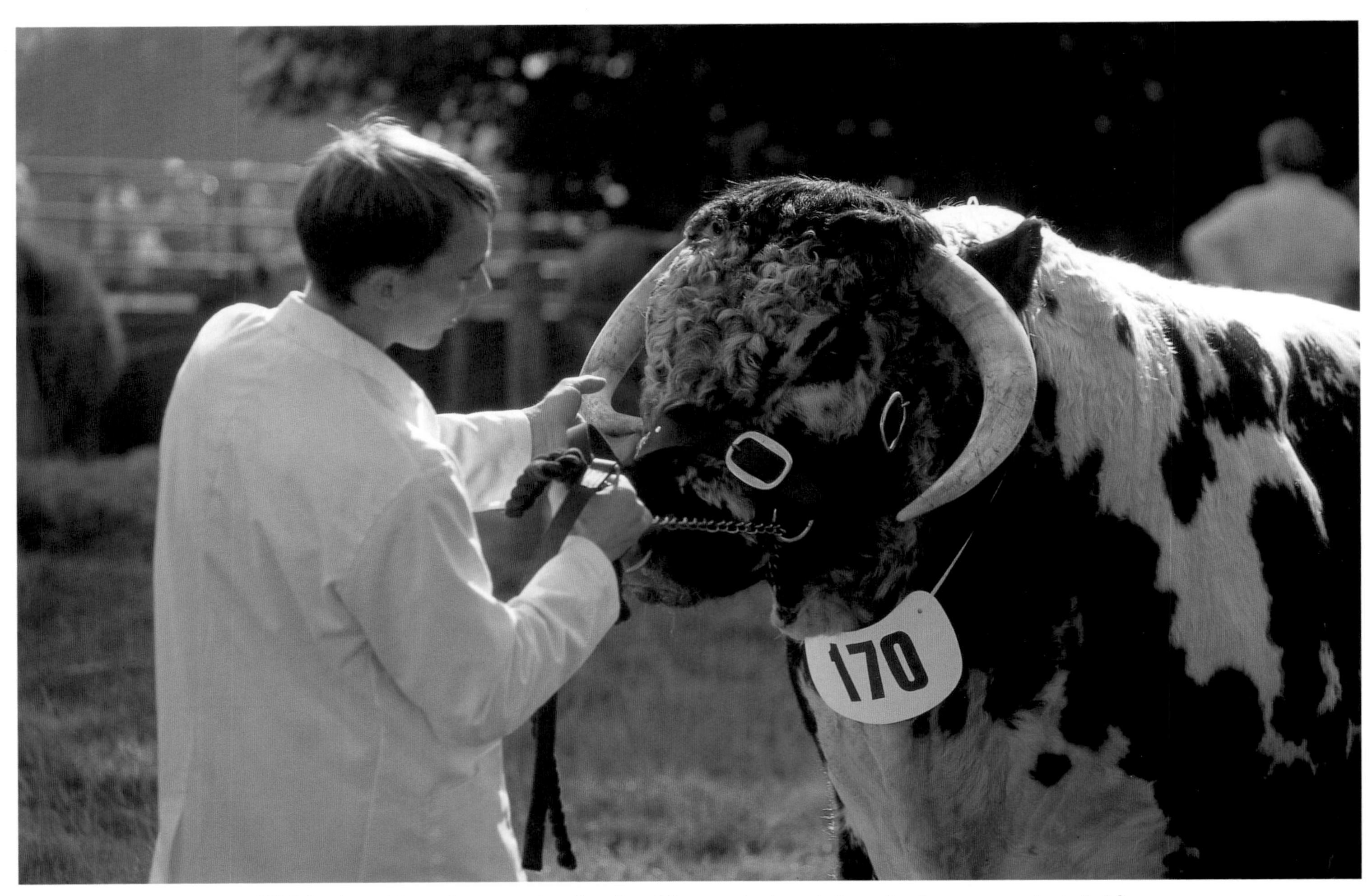

Wolsingham Show is reputed to be the oldest agricultural show in the country. It is held on the first weekend in September and attracts visitors from all over the country.

The road to the elephant trees. Bollihope Common, on the edge of Weardale is a pleasant upland moorland walk.

Stanhope Common in Weardale has a magnificent display of heather in bloom during late summer.

Stanhope Dene, carved out of the uplands by Stanhope Burn, was once heavily industrialised, but now offers quiet walks among the silent remains. Stanhope, pronounced 'Stannup', means 'rocky valley' and this is from where the nearby market town town takes its name.

The old trackbed of the Waskerley and the Weardale and Derwent railway was once the highest standard gauge railway in the county, but is now popular for cycling and walking. A trackside marker dating from the mid 1800s, carved with the initials of the famous Stockton and Darlington Railway, serves as a reminder of the time when they operated this busy line.

Steward Shield Meadow, an oasis of green on the high Weardale moorland.

Stanhope Common in winter – looking towards Steward Shield.

Stanhope Ford is an ancient crossing point on the River Wear – it presents no problem in low water but many motorists who have misjudged the depth and speed of the river at this point have had to be rescued, despite the prominent warning signs.

St Thomas' Church in Stanhope was once one of the richest in County Durham – not surprising when its parish once covered over 60000 acres.

Stanhope Agricultural show is usually held in September and provides an opportunity to proudly present the products of another year's hard work as well as provide a little fun and relaxation after the labours of harvest time.

Eastgate Sheep Show is held at the end of May. Fierce but friendly competition decides who has the best animals.

A dales farm near Rookhope – the evening light playing on the rich landscape of the hillsides can produce some beautiful effects.

The village of Rookhope was once the scene of much industrial activity but is now a sleepy dales village.

Rookhope Burn on a warm summer evening.

Rookhope Chimney Arch is almost all that remains of the massive lead-smelting mill that worked here during the Industrial Revolution. This huge chimney, the vertical flue of the mill, extended over 2500 yards up the hillside to a height of over 1800 feet where it belched out its noxious fumes. They were so bad that even today, over 100 years later, there is no vegetation at this point.

Bolts Law Incline and Winding House.
The winding house at Redgate Head at the top of Bolt's Law housed a huge stationary steam engine that hauled railway trucks over a mile up the steep incline to a height of over 500 feet.

Jeffrey's Chimney on the fells between Weardale and Derwentside serves as a reminder of when the North Pennine Lead Mining Industry was one of the biggest in the world.

Lime Kilns at White Kirkley, near Frosterley. Enormous amounts of 'mountain limestone' were quarried in Weardale and burned to provide quicklime for industry and agriculture.

Westerhopeburn Farm, near Eastgate, is one of the oldest farmhouses in Weardale and dates from 1606. It was once part of the huge estate belonging to the Hildyards who were a prominent family in the area for over 500 years.

A very cold, bright morning on the River Wear at Daddry Shield, Weardale.

The hay meadows of late spring and early summer are a mesmerising display of wildflowers and grasses. They are cut after they have seeded and the resulting fodder is stored for winter feed.

Greenfoot Quarry in late summer, the silent stillness is a great contrast to the days when it would have been working.

A horse enjoys the sweet taste of the summer flowers in a Weardale hay meadow.

Winter light produces an almost surreal effect at Westgate in Weardale.

High Mill is now a private home but once ground corn for the people of Westgate and the surrounding area.

Winter mist shrouds an old lead mining reservoir in the Middlehope Valley.

Trackways of old lead mining railways can still be seen in Slit Wood, athough they are now part of the landscape.

Eastgate and Westgate were once, literally, the gates to the Prince Bishops' Weardale hunting park. High Wesgate was the site of their substantial castle serving the park, although now there are only scant remains.

The River Wear tumbles over one of the many small waterfalls on its course near Ireshopeburn (pronounced 'aye-sup-burn') in Upper Weardale.

My son Mark and his labrador Archie at one of the ancient crossing points on the River Wear at Ireshopeburn.

A cottage on the fellside road near Newhouse – the bulge in the exterior wall below the chimney is evidence of a bread oven.

Late summer in Upper Weardale.

Looking westwards along Weardale from West Blackdene in summer.

Burnhope Reservoir and Upper Weardale in a fleeting moment of atmospheric light as seen from the old carriers' way on Race Head.

The Seeingsike Road in Weardale is an old drovers' road and recalls the days before the coming of the railways when livestock was driven to market on the hoof.

Race Head is the highest point on an old carriers' way which led from Sedling Rake Lead Mine to the smelt mill at Rookhope.

The confluence of Killhope and Burnhope Burns at Wearhead is the start of the River Wear which flows eastwards to Durham City, looping around the World Heritage Site of the Castle and Cathedral, and eventually into the North Sea at Sunderland.

Crossing Carr Brow Moor, Weardale, is a well-worn drovers' road, however these green ways were also used by salters, who, naturally, transported salt, broggers who were licenced to sell wool, and badgers who dealt in corn, as well as itinerant pedlars and tinkers who would wander from market to market plying their various trades.

Lanehead, Weardale. Cold harsh winters are common in the Pennine dales, although the snow transforms the landscape with an ethereal beauty.

Swaledale Sheep are hardy animals, a double coat keeps out the cold and the wet, and their constant foraging helps ensure their survival in harsh conditions.

Upper Weardale in winter. The swirling snow makes it hard to tell where the hills end and the sky begins. The beauty of the snow cover belies the fact that hill farming is an arduous, exhausting occupation in winter, a constant struggle against the vicious elements.

Killhope Lead Mining Centre is possibly the most complete lead mining site in Britain. Through authentic reconstruction it portrays an accurate account of the day-to-day lives of leadminers and their dangerous occupation. It also affords the opportunity to go underground as well as providing a chance to participate in many 'hands-on' tasks to complement the experience.

Raby Castle is perhaps one of the most impressive castles in County Durham. It is the family seat of the Lord Barnard whose estates reach as far south as Yorkshire and as far west as Cumbria. The castle once belonged to the Neville family but they lost their lands because of their shady involvement with 'The Rising of the North' – a plan to put Mary Queen of Scots, on the throne instead of Elizabeth I.

St Mary's Church, Staindrop, had its origins in Saxon times but was greatly enlarged and altered in the twelfth, thirteenth, and fourteenth centuries. It is the burial place of a succession of nobility who have resided in nearby Raby Castle.

Copley Chimney. This 115 feet high chimney is part of the remains of Copley Smelt Mill which operated from the late 1700s to the late 1800s and served the Teesdale lead mining fields. It was owned by the Lords of Raby who were entitled to a tythe of all the lead ore mined on their estates.

Hamsterley is the largest working forest in County Durham but still provides plenty of opportunity for leisure activities such as horse riding, cycling and walking.

The high, wild Pikestone Fell separates Weardale and Teesdale.

Bowes Museum at Barnard Castle was founded in the nineteenth century by John Bowes and his French wife, Josephine, to house their ever-increasing collection of treasures. Sadly they both died before it was opened to the public in 1892. Durham County Council took over the administration and running of the museum in 1956.

The original thirteenth-century Barnard Castle Bridge was destroyed in the Great Flood of 1771 after which the present one was built.

Barnard Castle, under the command of Sir George Bowes, once withstood a siege by 5000 men and artillery for ten days during the reign of Elizabeth I; however in the reign of Charles I it was extensively dismantled on the orders of Sir Henry Vane to provide material for the repair and rebuilding of Raby Castle.

Egglestone Abbey was founded towards the end of the twelfth century by Ralph de Multon for the White Canons of the Premonstratensian Order. The abbey became well known for its poverty brought on by unscheduled visits from both English and Scottish armies – in fact things were so bad they had to borrow £20 from the archbishop. Things went from bad to worse and by sixteenth century there were serious disciplinary complaints about the behaviour of the bretheren. The abbey was dissolved at the Reformation in 1540.

Eggleston hall was built by the distinguished Durham architect Ignatious Bonomi for William Hutchinson in about 1820.

The village green, Romaldkirk. St Romauld's Church is often referred to as 'the Cathedral of the Dales' and is built on the site of an early Saxon church. The village pump was in regular use until 1936.

The attractive village of Cotherstone, on the south bank of the River Tees is one of the few villages in County Durham that boasts its own cheese.

The Butter Stone on Cotherstone Moor is a fine example of a plague stone; marked as a place outside a stricken village where bartered goods or money would be left for exchange, to minimise the risk of infection.

Selset Reservoir in Lunedale, late on a warm summer evening.

Lunedale in early autumn.

Bowes Castle was built in 1170 for Henry II as a garrisoned outpost to guard the approach to Stainmore Pass – the main route in and out of Cumbria.

God's Bridge is a natural limestone bridge and carries a drovers' road
– now part of the Pennine Way – over the River Greta.

Baldersdale in spring – hay meadows on the banks of Blackton and Hury Reservoirs, with Goldsborough in the distance.

Mickle Fell in Lunedale is the highest fell in County Durham at 2591 feet.

Lead mining hushes are found all over the North Pennines. This was a popular way to extract lead ore in the eighteenth century. A stream would be dammed at the top of its valley until a good head of water built up – the dam would then be breached releasing a powerful torrent of water which would wash away the topsoil, allowing the miners to pick away the revealed lead ore. The process would be repeated along the valley of the stream until all the ore had been extracted.

A classic view along Teesdale from Whistle Crag.

Kirkcarrion high above Middleton-in-Teesdale. A stand of Scots Pines marks the burial mound of a celtic prince – Caryn – hence the name 'Caryn's Castle' or 'Kirkcarrion'. Legend has it that his tormented ghost wanders the fellside seeking revenge for the plundering of his tomb.

Autumn on the River Tees near Stoneygill, looking towards Crosthwaite Scars.

Looking from 'the Old Road' in Teesdale to Low Houses,
with Crosthaite Common rising in the distance.

Bowlees Beck – the Tees and its tributaries are reputed to have more waterfalls than any other river system in England.

Summerhill Force and Gibson's Cave, Bowlees in Teesdale. Gibson's cave, behind Summerhill Force, is where a sixteenth century outlaw, William Gibson, took refuge while he was being hunted by the Constable of Barnard Castle.

Walking through the hay meadows near Bowlees – the white-painted buildings signify that they are part of the vast Raby estate.

The Wynch Bridge spans the Tees just below Low Force. The original, which collapsed in 1720, was believed to be the first suspension bridge in Britain. The present bridge dates from 1830.

Low Force Falls are perhaps the most attractive on the Tees. Their old name was Salmon Leap Falls because of the huge number of fish that once worked their way upstream here – the old locals say that they caught so many that they 'carted them away by the barrer load!'

Holwick Scar –impressive crags of Whin Sill overlook the village of Holwick, Teesdale.

Sorting sheep. Swaledales are herded ready for the autumn sales.

Part of the The Pennine Way follows the River Tees from Middleton-in-Teesdale to Cauldron Snout. This is, in good weather, a pleasant and less strenuous section.

Early summer in Teesdale – the field barn provides an interesting contrast with the hay meadow.

High Force from 'The Yorkshire side' – at this point the south bank of the River Tees was in Yorkshire before the boundary changes in 1974.

High Force from 'The Durham side' – a footpath, well maintained by the Raby Estates, leads down to an excellent viewing point in front of the falls. Particularly heavy rain, combined with melt water from the fells causes the river to flow over both channels. These spectacular falls are over 80 feet high and are the biggest falls on any major river in England.

Upper Teesdale and Cronkley Scar in winter.

Upper Teesdale in summer looking across pasture to Cronkley Scar from Forest in Teesdale.

Langdon Beck, Teesdale, on a warm, golden summer evening.

Cronkley Farm is possibly one of the most remote farms in Teesdale.

The Pennine Way, at the base of Falcon Clints, is an uneven scramble over large boulders.

The shores of Cow Green Reservoir.

Early morning mist shrouds Cow Green reservoir in this winter view from Backside Fell.

Cow Green Reservoir in winter with Little Dun Fell, Great Dun Fell and Crossfell in the distance.

Spring gentian. This very rare alpine flower only grows in Upper Teesdale in County Durham.

The cascading fury of white water that is Cauldron Snout plunges over 200 yards from Cow Green to Falcon Clints.

The 'final plunge' in the words of Alfred Wainwright, the noted fellwalker, of the longest waterfall in England.

A freezing cold, misty morning in the remote Harwood Vale in Upper Teesdale.

Sunset over Crossfell, the highest point of the North Pennines.